A REPLY

TO

THE NATIONAL PAPER

ON

POSITIVISM.

BY

A POSITIVIST.

𝕮𝖆𝖑𝖈𝖚𝖙𝖙𝖆:

PRINTED BY I. C. BOSE & CO., STANHOPE PRESS, 172, BOW-BAZAR ROAD.

1868.

Price 1 Rupee.

PREFACE.

To those who have not read the articles in the *National Paper* the following sections may appear somewhat unconnected. A table has been supplied in order to show the order of arrangement at a glance : this table may, to some extent, obviate any occasional abruptness of transition.

We would wish it to be clearly understood that our object in writing this Reply is not to attack an adversary, but simply to explain, as far as our ability permits, what seems to us to be the correct Positivist view upon each point against which objections (more or less forcible) have been urged. Hence we trust that our arguments may be intelligible, even to those who have not read the articles in the *National Paper*.

CONTENTS.

A REPLY

TO

"THE NATIONAL" ON POSITIVISM.

———————◇———————

WE purpose in the following pages to consider some of the objections which have been lately brought against Positivism in the columns of *The National Paper*.

1. The writer observes " that Positivism, in its fully developed character, is the most determined enemy of Theism that has arisen during the 19th century." This we readily admit, but we cannot so readily agree with the writer when he immediately afterwards asserts that Positivism is "a most determined enemy of Hindoo *nationality*." As no arguments have been adduced in proof of this latter statement, we are at a loss to know upon what foundation it is based. Positivism, it appears to us, while aiming at unity, by no means discourages partial diversity—it aspires to found a universal doctrine it is true, but not to obliterate those broad demarcations which separate nation from nation and race from race. From the individual we advance to the family, from the family to the city, from the city to the nation, from the nation to the race: but as there are many individuals, and as each is endowed with a special idiosyncrasy ; so with the larger aggregates there are many distinct types, and whenever any one of these perishes, Humanity must be regarded as so much the poorer for the loss.

2. Speaking of Bacon, Descartes, Newton, and Galileo, it is said " none of the four considered the knowledge of causes beyond our reach—still less the knowledge of the Great First Cause." This statement is perfectly true, but it can in no way be regarded as a valid objection to Positivism. It is only since the time of Newton that Chemistry and Biology have been rendered thoroughly positive, and it was not till Comte had traced the laws of Sociology, (thus showing that the whole realm of human energy is subject to the same general order,) that the formation of a Positive Philosophy became possible. Bacon, Descartes, Newton and Galileo were positivists as men of science, but as philosophers they were, and could not help being,

metaphysicians: a Metaphysical *Philosophy* in their days was, the only possible one, (Theology having already been considerably weakened by the encroachments of science,) and the metaphysicians were destined to gain many a triumph ere it could become manifest that a new and better doctrine was needed to renovate the mind of man. *Science* is particular, but *Philosophy* is general; hence a philosophy, founded upon science, can only be introduced at that stage of human progress when *all* our conceptions have become thoroughly scientific. Those who accept Positivism believe that Comte has satisfactorily laid down the laws which govern human intelligence and action, and consequently that a Positive Philosophy is henceforward feasible—and being feasible, is destined, from its suitability to our mental and social necessities, to triumph completely over Theology and Metaphysics.

With reference to the terms in which Comte speaks of the non-religious character of modern astronomy, it may be allowed that the language employed is somewhat exaggerated: but it can scarcely be denied that in the present age we are more prone to trace the action of Providence in the mutable affairs of men, "the moving accidents by flood and field," than in the regular courses of the stars or in any other of the now-familiar celestial phenomena.*

3. The charge of Atheism which is generally brought against Comte, is to a certain extent a valid one. Positivism does not deny the existence of God, but then it does not assert that existence, and it strenuously opposes every endeavour to organize society upon any but a human basis. Comte objected to be called an atheist, because he regarded the atheistic school as a metaphysical one—since it pretended to afford a solution of the problems of ontology, by denying the existence of God and by asserting the eternity of matter. Comte thus describes the attitude of Positivism with reference to Atheism† :— "The fact of entire freedom from theological belief being necessary before the Positive state can be perfectly attained, has induced superficial observers to confound Positivism with a state of pure negation. Now this state was at one time, and that even so recently as the last century, favourable to progress; but at present in those who unfortunately still remain in it, it is a radical obstacle

---

* We do not think it necessary to notice what is said about Laplace, further than by observing that this great mathematician was an orthodox Catholic, and therefore not a member of any atheistic school : his Cosmogony has, perhaps, given rise to the notion that he was an unbeliever.

† General View of Positivism—Translated by Dr. J. H. Bridges. See p. 49.

to all sound, social, and even intellectual organisation. I have long ago repudiated all philosophical or historical connection between Positivism and what is called Atheism. But it is desirable to expose the error somewhat more clearly. Atheism, even from the intellectual point of view, is a very imperfect form of emancipation; for its tendency is to prolong the metaphysical stage indefinitely, by continuing to seek for new solutions of Theological problems, instead of setting aside all inaccessible researches on the ground of their utter inutility. The true Positive spirit consists in substituting the study of the invariable laws of phenomena, for that of their so-called causes, whether proximate or primary; in a word, in studying the *How* instead of the *Why*. Now this is wholly incompatible with the ambitions and visionary attempts of Atheism to explain the formation of the Universe, the origin of animal life, &c. The Positivist comparing the various phases of human speculation, looks upon these scientific chimeras as far less valuable even from the intellectual point of view than the first spontaneous inspirations of primeval times. The principle of Theology is to explain everything by supernatural *Wills*. That principle can never be set aside until we acknowledge the search for *Causes* to be beyond our reach, and limit ourselves to the knowledge of *Laws*. As long as men persist in attempting to answer the insoluble questions which occupied the attention of the childhood of our race, by far the more rational plan is to do as was done then, that is, simply to give free play to the imagination. These spontaneous beliefs have gradually fallen into disuse, not because they have been disproved, but because mankind has become more enlightened as to its wants and the scope of its powers, and has gradually given an entirely new direction to its speculative efforts. If we insist upon penetrating the unattainable mystery of the essential cause that produces phenomena, there is no hypothesis more satisfactory than that they proceed from Wills dwelling in them or outside them; an hypothesis which assimilates them to the effect produced by the desires which exist within ourselves. Were it not for the pride induced by metaphysical and scientific studies, it would be inconceivable that any theist, modern or ancient, should have believed that his vague hypotheses on such a subject were preferable to this direct mode of explanation. And it was the only mode which really satisfied the reason, until men began to see the utter inanity and inutility of all search for absolute truth. The Order of Nature is doubtless very imperfect in every respect; but its production is far more compatible with the hypothesis of an intelligent Will than with that of a blind mechanism. Persistent atheists therefore would seem to be the most illogical of theologists : because they occupy themselves with theological problems, and yet reject the only appropriate method of handling them. But the fact is that pure Atheism, even in the present day, is very rare. What is called Atheism, is usually a phase of Pantheism which is nothing but a relapse, disguised under learned terms, into a vague and abstract form of Fetichism. And it is not impossible that it may lead to the re-production in one form or other of every theological phase, as soon as the check which modern society still imposes on metaphysical extravagance, has become somewhat weakened. The adoption of such theories as a satisfactory system of belief, indicates a very exaggerated or rather false view of intellectual requirements, and a very insufficient recognition of moral and social wants. It is generally connected with the visionary but mischievous tendencies of ambitious thinkers to uphold what they call the empire of Reason. In the moral sphere, it forms a sort of basis for the degrading fallacies of modern metaphysicians as to the absolute preponderance of self-interest. Politically its tendency is to unlimited prolongation of the revolutionary position, its spirit is that of blind hatred to the past : and it resists all attempts to explain it on Positive principles, with the view of disclosing the future. Atheism, therefore, is not likely to lead to Positivism except in those who pass through it rapidly as the last and most short-lived of metaphysical phases. Negation offers but a feeble and precarious basis for union : and disbelief in Monotheism is of itself no better proof of a mind fit to grapple with the questions of the day than disbelief in Polytheism or Fetichism, which no one would maintain to be an adequate ground for claiming intellectual sympathy. The atheistic phase indeed was not really necessary, except for the revolutionists of the last century, who took the lead in the movement towards a radical regeneration of society. The necessity has already ceased; for the decayed condition of the old system makes the need of regeneration palpable to all. Persistence in anarchy, and Atheism is the most characteristic symptom of anarchy, is a temper of mind more unfavourable to the organic spirit, which ought by this time to have established its influence, than sincere adhesion to the old forms. This latter is of course obstructive : but at least it does not hinder us from fixing our attention upon the great social problem. Indeed it helps us to do so : because it forces the new philosophy to throw aside every weapon of attack against the older faith except its own higher capacity of satisfying our moral and social wants.

but in the Atheism maintained by many metaphysicians and scientific men of the present day, Positivism, instead of wholesome rivalry of this kind, will meet with nothing but barren resistance. Anti-theological, as such men may be, they feel unmixed repugnance for any attempts at social regeneration, although their efforts in the last century had to some extent prepared the way for it."

Hence it is clear that Positivism, although hostile to Deism, as a scientific hypothesis, and rejecting it as a definitive belief, nevertheless ready to welcome it as affording a provisional synthesis and as constituting a preliminary basis for social regeneration. In India no doubt Deism, under some form or other, must prevail for years to come—the popular mind being still polytheistic, while the educated classes are, as a rule, essentially metaphysical.—It cannot be expected that Positivism would attract any but a few select thinkers, until the metaphysical doctrines have been thoroughly tested—socially as well as intellectually—and have been found wanting. When the chaos, which must ever result from any attempt to organise with revolutionary beliefs, has become painfully manifest, then it may be expected that *all* who prefer unity to schism, order to confusion, peace to discord, and who have the true welfare of their country at heart, will be ready to give up the eidola of the past, and to welcome a system which is truly organic, and which merely recommends us to resign ourselves to an inevitable ignorance regarding the mysteries of creation in order that it may replace that ignorance by a fruitful knowledge of human powers and human necessities.

4. But Comte has not only been charged with Atheism : it is so commonly alleged that he belongs to a materialistic school of philosophy. Here again we must point out a misconception, because, whatever may be the opinion of this or that individual regarding the tendencies of Positivism as a whole, it must be remembered that the term 'materialism' has become connected with a definite body of doctrine which is thoroughly alien to the Positive view, and which Comte strenuously endeavoured to overthrow. In answering this charge we shall, as before, allow Comte to speak for himself*:—"The charge of Materialism which is often made against Positive philosophy, is of more importance (than that of Atheism). It originates in the course of scientific study upon which the Positive system is based. In answering the charge need not enter into any discussion of impenetrable mysteries.

* 'General View of Positivism.'—Translated by Dr. J. H. Bridges. See p. 52.

Our theory of development will enable us to see distinctly the real ground of the confusion that exists upon the subject. Positive science was for a long time limited to the simplest subjects; it could not reach the highest except by a natural series of intermediate steps. As each of these steps is taken, the student is apt to be influenced too strongly by the methods and results of the preceding stage. Here, as it seems to me, lies the real source of that scientific error which men have instinctively blamed as *materialism*. The name is just, because the tendency indicated is one which degrades the higher subjects of thought by confounding them with the lower. It was hardly possible that this usurpation by one science of the domain of another should have been wholly avoided. For, since the more special phenomena do really depend upon the more general, it is perfectly legitimate for each science to exercise a certain deductive influence upon that which follows it in the scale. By such influence the special inductions of that science were rendered more coherent. The result, however, is that each of the sciences has to undergo a long struggle against the encroachments of the one preceding it ; a struggle which even in the case of the subjects which have been studied longest, is not yet over. Nor can it entirely cease until the controlling influence of sound philosophy be established over the whole scale, introducing juster views of the relations of its several parts, about which at present there is such irrational confusion. Thus it appears that Materialism is a danger inherent in the mode in which the scientific studies, necessary as a preparation for Positivism, were pursued. Each science tended to absorb the one next to it, on the ground of having reached the Positive stage earlier and more thoroughly. The evil then is really deeper and more extensive than is imagined by most of those who deplore it. It passes generally unnoticed except in the higher class of subjects. These doubtless are more seriously affected, inasmuch as they undergo the encroaching process from all the rest ; but we find the same thing in different degrees, in every step of the scientific scale. Even the lowest step, Mathematics, is no exception, though its position would seem at first sight to exempt it. To a philosophic eye there is Materialism in the common tendency of mathematicians at the present day to absorb Geometry or Mechanics into the Calculus, as well as in the more evident encroachments of Mathematics upon Physics, of Physics upon Chemistry, of Chemistry, which is more frequent, upon Biology, or lastly in the common tendency of the best biologists to look upon Sociology as a mere corollary of their own science. In all these cases it is the same fundamental error: that is, an exaggerated use of deductive reasoning; and in all it is attended with the same result: that the higher studies are in constant danger of being disorganised by the indiscriminate application of the lower. All scientific specialists at the present time are more or less materialists, according as the phenomena they study are more or less simple and general. Geometricians, therefore, are more liable to the error than any others; they all aim, consciously or otherwise, at a synthesis in which the most elementary studies, those of number, space, and motion, are made to regulate all the rest. But the biologists who resist this encroachment most energetically, are often guilty of the same mistake. They not unfrequently attempt, for instance, to explain all sociological facts by the influence of climate and race, which are purely secondary; thus showing their ignorance of the fundamental laws of Sociology, which can only be discovered by a series of direct inductions from history.

" This philosophical estimate of Materialism explains how it is that it has been brought as a charge against Positivism, and at the same time proves the deep injustice of the charge. Positivism, far from countenancing so dangerous an error, is, as we have seen, the only philosophy which can completely remove it. The error arises from certain tendencies which are in themselves legitimate, but which have been carried too far; and Positivism satisfies these tendencies in their due measure. Hitherto the evil has remained unchecked, except by the theologico-metaphysical spirit, which, by giving rise to what is called spiritualism, has rendered a very valuable service. But useful as it has been, it could not arrest the active growth of Materialism, which has assumed in the eyes of modern thinkers something of a progressive character, from having been so long connected with the cause of resistance to a retrograde system. Notwithstanding all the protests of the spiritualists, the lower sciences have encroached upon the higher to an extent that seriously impairs their independence and their value. But Positivism meets the difficulty far more effectually. It satisfies and reconciles all that is really tenable in the rival claims of both Materialism and Spiritualism; and, having done this, it discards them both. It holds the one to be as dangerous to Order as the other to Progress. This result is an immediate consequence of the establishment of the encyclopædic scale, in which each science retains its own proper sphere of induction, while deductively it remains subordinate to the science which precedes it. But what really decides the matter is the fact that such paramount importance, both logically and scientifically, is given by Positive

Philosophy to social questions. For these are the questions in which the influence of Materialism is most mischievous, and also in which it is most easily introduced. A system, therefore, which gives them the precedence over all other questions, must hold Materialism to be quite as obstructive as Spiritualism, since both are alike an obstacle to the progress of that science, for the sake of which all other sciences are studied. Further advance in the work of social regeneration implies the elimination of both of them, because it cannot proceed without exact knowledge of the laws of moral and social phenomena.

"With the view of securing a dispassionate consideration of this subject, and of avoiding all confusion, I have laid no stress upon the charge of immorality that is so often brought against Materialism. The reproach, even when made sincerely, is constantly belied by experience. Indeed it is inconsistent with all that we know of human nature. Our opinions, whether right or wrong, have not, fortunately, the absolute power over our feelings and conduct which is commonly attributed to them. Materialism has been provisionally connected with the whole movement of emancipation, and it has therefore often been found in common with the noblest aspirations. That connection, however, has now ceased ; and it must be owned that even in the most favourable cases this error, purely intellectual though it be, has to a certain extent always checked the free play of our nobler instincts, by leading men to ignore or misconceive moral phenomena, which were left unexplained by its crude hypothesis."

5. When Mr. Mill asserts that it is " compatible with the Positive Philosophy to believe that the universe was created and even that it is continuously governed by an Intelligence, provided we admit that the Intelligent Governor adheres to fixed laws," it appears to us that he mistakes the spirit of the philosophy which he professes to interpret. Such an hypothesis is purely metaphysical, and as the conception of creation is one which our human faculties cannot realise, Positivism dismisses it— accepting the mystery, but refusing to pretend that it can withdraw the solemn veil which conceals that mystery. Those who believe that God has revealed his existence and providential action to certain chosen organs of the human race, can claim the right to furnish a solution of problems whose depths our unaided reason can never sound ; but those theists who discard the gospel of any inspired prophet, who regard the sons of men as all on the same intellectual level, all sharing in the same common stock of intuitions—can speak with no authority, can set up no generally recognised arbiter to decide between contending

tions : their principle is not organic, and after struggling on a while with a precarious life, must either yield to the old ology or bow before the triumph of a doctrine of humanity.

When it is said that the laws which are the object of positive earch "have no origin, have no superior will to control them, 1 no beginning, and can have no end, cannot be reversed, opended or interfered with by God, no more than by man. ey are consequently necessary, immutable, eternal, indepen- nt of God and man," it must be remembered that the writer ieducing his own consequences, and not alleging the opinions Comte who always consistently persevered in his determin- on never to examine the metaphysical bearings of his doctrines.* ecessary' 'eternal' and 'immutable' are terms which do not enter o the Positive Vocabulary.

5. With reference to the doctrine of Final Causes. We shall t state, in brief, Comte's opinion as to the influence of astro- ny on this doctrine. "Astronomy," according to Comte "has e more than any other pursuit—simply because it is the most entific of all—to expose and destroy the doctrine of final causes, ich is generally regarded by the moderns as the basis of every igious system, though it is in fact a consequence and not a ise. The knowledge of the motion of the earth has overthrown very foundation of the doctrine, which supposed the universe be subordinated to our globe, and therefore to man. Since when's time, the development of celestial mechanics has depriv- taeological philosophy of its principal intellectual office, by wing that the order maintained throughout our system and whole universe is by the simple gravitation of its parts. If took an *à priori* view, we should say that, as we exist, our tem must be such as to admit of our existence ; and one essary condition of this is such a degree of stability in our tem as we actually find. This stability we scientifically per- ve to be a simple consequence of mechanical laws working ong the incidents of our system,—the extremely small plane- y bodies in their relation to the larger sun ; the small eccen- ity of their orbits, and moderate inclination of their planes ; ich incidents, again, are necessary consequences of the mode of mation of the entire system. The stability by virtue of which hold our existence is not found in the case of comets, whose

---

* Having clearly exhibited the inutility of all metaphysical speculation, it was likely that he would stultify himself by discussing his principles from a aphysical point of view. It was sufficient for him that his doctrines should ish a stable basis for human action ; their suitability to man's needs would ish their strongest claim to be generally accepted.

perturbations are not only great, but liable to indefinite increase, and their being inhabited is inconceivable. Thus, the doctrine of final causes would be reduced to the truism that there are no inhabited bodies in our system but those which are habitable. This brings us back to the principle of the conditions of existence, which is the true positive transformation of the doctrine of final causes, and of far superior scope and profit in every way."

The doctrine of final causes is rejected by Positivism, not because it is incapable of leading to trustworthy conclusions, but because it is an hypothesis which cannot be verified and which is quite as likely to lead the mind astray as to direct it into right paths. The doctrine has, ere now, given rise (as in the case of Harvey's discovery of the circulation of the blood) to important and valuable results, but it was never very fruitful, and as it erred against the fundamental conditions of a true scientific hypothesis, Positivism, it appears to us, has done well in replacing it by the principle of ' the conditions of existence'— a principle in every way superior to the metaphysical figment which it seeks to supplant.

In Natural Theology the doctrine of final causes, under the form of ' the argument from design,' is employed to prove the existence of God. As Positivists we are loath to enter upon any metaphysical discussion, but it may be observed that this celebrated argument can do no more than prove a Demiurgus, it cannot bridge over the mighty chasm between existence and non-existence, it can never show how something was evolved out of nothing, and therefore can never lead man's mind from the creature up to the *Creator*. There is no analogy between the creation of matter and its simple modification which is all that man can effect, and the only formative process of which he can form any rational idea.

The Natural Theologian is virtually forced to give up the Omnipotence of God, though he endeavours to save his dogma by making the Deity impose limits upon his own power. " Whatever is done," says Paley, " God could have done without the intervention of instruments or means ; but it is in the construction of instruments, in the choice and adaptation of means, that a creative intelligence is seen. It is this which constitutes the order and beauty of the universe. God, therefore, has been pleased to prescribe limits to his own power, and to work his ends within those limits. * * * * It has been said that the problem of creation was, " attraction and matter being given, to make a world out of them ; " and, as above explained, this statement perhaps does not convey a false idea."—Laws

work by, and matter to work upon, are necessary pas-
al to, however much metaphysicians may attempt to disguise
the mental impotence which renders them essential. Once grant
these postulates unreservedly, and the whole fabric of Ontology is
dissolved.—Revelation may indeed survive the wreck, but men in
general will give little heed to systems which reposing neither on
Reason nor on Faith, are unable to satisfy their most urgent
mental and social requirements.

In contemplating the works of nature, the presence of design—
the adaptation of certain means to certain ends—is supposed to
furnish us with a knowledge of several attributes of the Deity,
and to teach us especially the divine goodness. Now it appears
to us, as it has appeared to others, that the operations of nature
may suggest other lessons besides those of inflexible justice and
supreme benevolence. The poet when meditating upon God and
Nature, the glorious hope of man and the mocking irony of fate,
thus mournfully exclaims :—*

> Are God and Nature then at strife
> That Nature lends such evil dreams ?
> So careful of the type she seems,
> So careless of the single life.
>
> ' So careful of the type ?' but no.
> From scarped cliff and quarried stone
> She cries ' a thousand types are gone'
> I care for nothing, all shall go.
>
> Thou makest thine appeal to me :
> I bring to life, I bring to death :
> The spirit does but mean the breath :
> I know no more.'————————

The same arguments derived from the *natural* world "which
prove that God is the author of food, light and life, prove him
also to be the author of poison, darkness and death.† The wide-
wasting earthquake, the storm, the battle, and the tyranny, are
(in the sphere of natural religion) attributable to Him in the same
degree as the fairest forms of nature, sunshine, liberty, and
peace."

Bacon saw clearly enough, even in his day, that final causes,
must be eventually expelled from the domain of science, though
he would have retained them in Theology and Metaphysics—
subjects whose complete overthrow could not at that period have

---

* Tennyson " In Memoriam."—We are aware that the poet manages to find an
swer to his doubts. He finds it, however, not in the open courts of Nature's
solemn temple but in the hidden sanctuary ' behind the veil.'
† Shelley, Note 12 to " Queen Mab."

been even dimly foreseen. Final causes, says Bacon in his *Novum Organum*, "have relation clearly to the nature of man rather than to the nature of the universe; and from this source have strangely defiled philosophy." This is only another mode of expressing the fact that such hypotheses are purely subjective, they rest upon no external basis and, therefore, do not admit of verification : they may lead to correct results, but it is certain that they have far oftener led to erroneous ones, and as it is impossible to tell beforehand whether they can be thoroughly relied on, it is best entirely to discard such treacherous weapons from the armoury of science.‡

M. Littré, in his preface to the 'Positive Philosophy,' has thus clearly and forcibly expressed the Positive view with reference to the doctrine of Final Causes :—" Positive science, which adheres to whatever is serviceable and dismisses all that is useless, has not always manifested an aversion for final causes, nor has it always regarded the hypothesis of a plan and design in the works of nature as contrary to its spirit. There was a time when, like metaphysics, it allowed these causes and this hypothesis to interfere in its researches ; but it soon perceived that no assistance could be derived from a doctrine which necessitated on the one hand a *first cause* whose nature could not be determined, and on the other a *purpose* which it was impossible to grasp. Hence science was compelled to have recourse to the fruitful principle of the conditions of existence—*fruitful* because it is relative and amenable to experiment. In practice we all, whether believers or unbelievers, renounce the first method and adhere to the second. According to strict logic, the doctrine of final causes ought to have been a result and not a principle; but this has been reversed, for the doctrine was established as a principle while the constitution of the world was but little

---

‡ Bacon has dwelt at some length on the nature of final causes, in the ' Advancement of Learning' B. III. ch. 4. He there says, " the handling of final causes in physics has driven away and overthrown the diligent inquiry of physical causes, and made men stay upon these specious and shadowy causes, without actively pressing the inquiry of those which are really and truly physical ; to the great arrest and prejudice of science. For to introduce such causes as these, " that the hairs of the eyelids are for a quickset and fence about the sight ;" or " that the firmness of the skins and hides of living creatures is to defend them from the extremities of heat and cold ;" or " that the bones are for columns or beams, whereupon the frames of the bodies of living creatures are built ;" or " that the leaves of trees are for protecting the fruit from the sun and wind ;" or " that the clouds are formed above for watering the earth ;" or " that the thickness and solidity of the earth is for the station and mansion of living creatures," and the like, is a proper inquiry in Metaphysics, but in Physics it is impertinent."

In B. III. ch. 5, he observes that " the inquisition of Final Causes is barren, and like a virgin consecrated to God produces nothing."

wn, and now that we are considerably wiser, it eagerly claims
t science should consecrate it as a result. Evidently, this
ception is *purely subjective*, or, which amounts to the same
g, metaphysical, and consequently it cannot be verified with
tainty.

In order to verifiy such a conception it must be ascertained
ther the supposed final purpose extends to the whole body
phenomena, or whether it allows certain categories to escape.
the first case, the hypothesis becomes a general fact ; in the
ond case, the contradiction between the different categories
phenomena becomes insoluble, the hypothesis unverifiable,
the pursuit unprofitable.

One of the best examples in favour of a final cause is that
the eye. The eye is an instrument, and an optician, in
workshop, would imitate it in arranging the various
dia, the curvature of the crystalline lens, the aperture of
pupil, in order that a distinct image might be projected on
retina. Hence it is natural to conclude " that an intelligent
se has had before itself the particular effect which each of
se parts separately ought to produce, and also the common
ct which they should produce when combined ;" in other words-
t this cause has had a plan, and has proposed to itself an end,
ich it has attained. Be it so : here then is an hypothesis
ified in this and in all analogous cases ; but it is not
wable to make a choice, it is necessary that we should
mine how the doctrine acquits itself with reference to
er conditions. The following is one instance which may be
ected from many such. The saliva of the dog is generally
rmless, but, by a chemico-vital process which has hitherto
ded the subtlety of human art, there is sometimes formed in
s saliva a deleterious principle, which proves fatal to the
mal itself and to all who are inoculated by means of its
e. But this is not all, for the new condition in which the animal
placed inspires it with a deadly desire to bite, so that the
se which has produced the poison, has, at the same time,
anged all the circumstances in such a manner that it should
be lost without causing extensive injury. What are we to say
this singular final cause ? And how is the purpose which ap-
rs to govern this case, to be reconciled with the purpose which
ears to govern the case of the eye ?"

To the same effect is the following passage from Dr. Maudsley's
hysiology and Pathology of the Mind *:'—" The notion that
soul works unconsciously in the building up of the organism,

---

* See chap. III, page 65.

which has at different times been so much in fashion, rests entirely upon the assumption that an intelligent principle or agent must be immanent in organic matter which is going through certain definite changes. But if in the formation of an organ, why not also in the formation of a chemical compound with its definite properties? The function is the necessary result of a certain definite organic structure under certain conditions, and in that sense must needs minister to the furtherance of its well-being. But an organic action, with never so beautifully manifest a design, may, under changed conditions, become as disastrous as it is usually beneficial; the peristaltic movements of the intestines, which serve so essential a purpose in the economy, may, and actually do, in the case of some obstruction, become the cause of intolerable suffering and a painful death. Where, then, is the design of their disastrous continuance? Whatever design we recognise is really an idea that is gradually formed in our minds from repeated experiences of the law of the matter."

7. The problem of Causation is one of those which Positivism does not attempt to solve. It is rejected because, as in the case of all metaphysical questions, contradictory solutions are given by opposite schools. These contradictory solutions cannot both be true, yet unfortunately there is no criterion, no means of verification, which can lead us to prefer one to the other. We are forced, therefore, to reject them both and to pronounce such investigations as beyond the reach of our faculties.

The so-called principle of causation implies that the cause and the effect are, to a certain extent, homogeneous, *the cause* being itself an effect with reference to prior causes, and *the effect* being itself a cause with reference to subsequent effects—hence the *First Cause*, if deduced from this principle, must be not a creative cause, which bears no analogy to the causes of which we have any experience, but a cause which might be an effect, and which, therefore, itself demands a cause quite as much as the effects which it is supposed to initiate.

Given A the cause and B the effect, we know that B must either follow or accompany A, but what the hidden nexus may be which establishes between A and B the relationship of cause and effect it is impossible for us to determine. We may say that the cause has a *potency* to produce the effect; but this explains nothing, it merely transfers to the phenomena a figment of our own minds; and leaves us, for all practical purposes, as wise as we were at first. Constant and orderly change is all that the external world really discloses to us. While the laws which govern the universe are still undetected man, not improperly, transfers his own desires and impulses to the objects which surround him, animates matter with a life analogous to his own, and thus introduces a fictitious unity which serves well enough for the provisional colligation of facts and interpretation of phenomena. These primitive views are marked by an overwhelming preponderance of the subjective element, a preponderance which at first is inevitable, but which every step in advance tends to diminish. As knowledge increases, we see more and more clearly the fictitious nature of our earlier assumptions; the arbitrary and unverifiable elements are gradually displaced till at length they are entirely relegated to a shadowy region of their own—the *domus exilis* of metaphysical abstractions.—Yet the imposing fabric whose foundations were laid during the dawn of speculation is not doomed to perish leaving man uncompensated for its loss. We must, it is true, resign ourselves to a certain ignorance, we must bring ourselves to confess that the secret agencies of nature will for ever elude our mental grasp, but while doing so we shall be richly rewarded for our submission, and the seeds which have hitherto produced but a scanty crop will henceforward bring forth fruit, some thirty, some sixty, some an hundred-fold. Giving up the sterile search after causes, let us gladly recognise the presence of universal law and direct all our energies to the ascertainment of *how* nature works in her manifold processes, for no otherwise can man realise the 'crescent promise' of his youth, and attain to a knowledge which is truly synonymous with power.

The manner in which the human mind advances from its primitive to its ultimate conceptions, is thus well described by Mr. G. H. Lewes, in his treatise on Aristotle. At first, "we animate Nature with intentions like our own. We derive our ideas of cause, and force, from our own experience of effort; and the changes we observe are interpreted as similar in origin to the changes we effect. This leads to the Fetichism of savages and children; to the Polytheism of more advanced intelligence; and, by a gradual refinement in abstraction, to the Metaphysics and Transcendental Physics of later days. We first impersonate the causes as Deities; we next eliminate more and more of the personal elements, leaving only abstract entities; we finally reduce these Entities to Forces, as the general expression of Properties or Relations; e. g. the Force of gravity is only the abstract expression of the fundamental relation which matter universally manifests. All matter is heavy; all masses attract other masses; this property is as universal and fundamental as that of impenetrability; we abstract it as gravitation or attraction. In this gradation the Will first disappears; next the independent Existence; leaving finally an abstract expression of observed order. In the final stage we recognise that what was assumed to be an independent something, regulating phenomena, moulding them according to *its* nature, is only an impersonation of the order in phenomena, the statement in abstract terms of the very facts themselves. Thus, observing the facts of organic growth and development, physiologists have attributed them to the agency of a Plastic Force, which moulds the heterogeneous elements into definite shapes. If, however, we seriously consider what this Plastic Force can be, *apart* from the phenomena, we are quickly led to perceive that it is only a name assigned to the observed order, a generalised expression of the facts, which has been personified, according to a well-known tendency."

8. There are, according to Comte, three methods of philosophising—(1) the *Theological*, (2) the *Metaphysical*, (3) the *Positive.*

It is easy to take objection to the phraseology here employed, but history reveals clearly enough the existence of three distinct methods, call them by what names we may. In the earlier stages of man's history there cannot be a doubt that society was mainly organised on a basis of supernaturalism, and that for a while there was a complete harmony between the different elements of human nature. But the incompatibility between the primitive or (as it is termed by Comte) theological hypothesis and the exigencies of practical life soon became manifest. Theology asserted all phenomena to be under the dominion of Wills more or less arbitrary; whereas in practical life men were led more and more clearly to the conception of invariable Laws.* Hence the primitive method undergoes a gradual transformation, the realm of Law being constantly increased by fresh annexations, while that of arbitrary Will is continually restricted and modified. But as it would be impossible to pass at once from the notion that the phenomena presented by the universe are governed either by an immanent or external will, to the notion of invariable laws,—written in characters that may be decyphered though the hand that traced them can never be discerned—a transition doctrine was needed, which should be neither wholly Theological nor wholly Positive, but which should partake of the characteristics of both these methods. Such a doctrine was furnished by what Comte has termed the Metaphysical Philosophy, in which the personal and purely human

---

* See 'Comte's General View of Positivism' by Dr. J. H. Bridges, p. 10.

icious of the primitive Theology are replaced by impersonal entities and shadowy abstractions, which are sufficiently vague to lull the suspicions of unwary theologists and at the same time to encourage the insidious advances of positive science.

The Theological and the Metaphysical philosophies resemble each other so far as they commence with the study of Man, and then proceed to the study of the external world : and in this respect they both equally differ from the Positive philosophy which proceeds inversely, namely, from the study of external nature to that of man ; always, however, keeping in view the ultimate reconciliation of the two methods. "If the consideration of man is to prevail over that of the universe, all phenomena are inevitably attributed to *will*,—first natural, and then outside of nature ; and this constitutes the theological system. On the contrary, the direct study of the universe suggests and developes the great idea of the *laws* of nature, which is the basis of all positive philosophy, and capable of extension to the whole of phenomena, including at last those of man and society. The one point of agreement among all schools of theology and metaphysics, which otherwise differ without limit, is that they regard the study of Man as primary, and that of the universe as secondary,—usually neglecting the latter entirely. Whereas, the most marked characteristic of the positive school is that it founds the study of Man on the prior knowledge of the external world."*

Pure (as distinguished from *metaphysical*) Theology manifests itself under three distinct forms—Fetichism, Polytheism, and Monotheism—to each of which there corresponds a peculiar regime and a characteristic philosophy or conception of the *universe*.† It would be out of place here to enter into any detail regarding these sub-divisions ; all that is required, for our present purpose, being, to indicate summarily their position in the history of man's development.

9. "Fetichism," says the writer in the *National*, "is a *Religion* not a *Theology*, nor a *Philosophy*." Now with Comte, Fetichism signifies a certain phase of human belief, (namely, the primitive theological phase,) which is distinguished by a peculiar *Philosophy* and *Religion*. From a philosophical point of view Fetichism conceives all external bodies to be animated by a life analogous to the life of man, with mere differences of intensity.

---

* 'Comte's Positive Philosophy' by Miss Martineau, vol. I. p. 356.
† We include in this term both *man* and *nature*.

Its religion, like all other religions, aimed at regulating man's individual nature, and at organising a community by furnishing a rallying point for its separate members. The grand object of religion, at all times and under all circumstances, is to secure that *unity* which is the distinctive mark of man's existence, both individual and social, and which can only be thoroughly realised when all the constituent parts of our nature, moral as well as physical, are made habitually to converge towards one common purpose.

10. It will be observed that the term 'Theology,' as employed by Comte, has a wide signification, including every phase of belief from Fetichism—in which the supernatural pervades all nature,—to simple Theism,—in which the Deity has almost vanished into a metaphysical abstraction. Theism in fact has far more affinity with Metaphysics than with Theology: its whole spirit is thoroughly metaphysical, but it borrows just enough from pure theology to give its doctrines a consistency which they would not otherwise possess, and thus to secure for its followers a partial discipline, and a certain principle of unity. Hence we are not inclined altogether to disagree with the writer in the *National* when he asserts that "the Theology of Theists, so far as it is a philosophical method, is really and truly Metaphysics, as the latter word is understood by Comte," and we are willing to allow that the purely subjective portions of the Metaphysical Philosophy are quite as fictitious as the conceptions of Theology, but with a difference,—for the latter are endowed with a vast organising power while there is no metaphysical system the complete doctrines of which are accepted in the same sense by even a dozen individuals.

11. The writer in the *National*, like many others who have criticised Comte, objects to the term 'Positivism.' The name, it appears to us, indicates tolerably well what Comte wished to express, namely, a system which rests merely upon ascertained facts and verifiable hypotheses, as distinct from systems which build upon purely subjective foundations, and which deal largely with certain ideas—the contradictories of notions derived from sense-experience. Thus while Science works with such materials as Number, Time, Space, Matter, Life, Law, &c.; Metaphysics, on the contrary, discusses Infinity, Eternity, the Unlimited, the Immaterial, Immortality, the Unconditioned, &c. We leave it to our readers to judge for themselves which of these two methods

of inquiry is likely to be most productive of real, or as Comte would term it *positive*, knowledge.*

The term ' Phenomenalism,' which the writer in the *National* suggests instead of ' Positivism,' has a special and limited connotation; it could not, therefore, without doing violence to established usage, have been employed by Comte to include the whole sphere of meaning which he has attached to the term ' Positivism'—a term which, being little in use before Comte's time, was well adapted to receive an extended signification. We cannot agree with the writer in the *National* in regarding either ' Natural Science' or ' The Philosophy of Science' as in any way equivalent expressions for the wide and suggestive name Positivism, which includes Natural Science and much more; which—as a Philosophy—is based upon science, it is true, but upon this basis it establishes a doctrine embracing all the phenomena of which our life consists—our thoughts, our feelings, and our actions.

When it is said that Positivism ignores *practice*, it appears to us that the scope and spirit of the system must have been thoroughly mistaken. It cannot be repeated too often that Comte's aim was not to build another temple to Science, nor to augment the blind worship already paid so largely at her altars, but to found a doctrine which should assign to science its proper place in the discipline of man, by making it instrumental in co-ordinating the whole sphere of human nature—intellectual, social, and moral.—" Positivism" Comte tells us,† " consists essentially of a Philosophy and a Polity. These can never be dissevered ; the former being the basis, and the latter the end of one comprehensive system, in which our intellectual faculties and our social sympathies are brought into close relation with each other." Again he says "the new general doctrine aims at something more than satisfying the Intellect ; it is in reality quite as favourable to Feeling and even to Imagination."

12. It is easy enough to cast ridicule upon many of the details of Comte's religious scheme. We are not among those who think that such details have much chance of being generally

---

* Positivism destroys it is true, but it destroys only in order that it may replace. *Metaphysics* in theology and *Democracy* in politics are both purely negative ; the former acting as a solvent of all organic belief, while the latter endeavours to secure progress by measures which are wholly anarchical. *Positivism*, on the other hand, aims at the reconstruction of religion by placing it upon an ascertained basis of science, and seeks the continuous improvement of mankind by establishing an order of which progress shall be the legitimate result.

† ' Comte's General View of Positivism' by Dr. Bridges p. 1.

accepted, though it is not impossible that a strong enthusiasm might induce large communities to receive much that now appears to us exaggerated and grotesque. It is most likely indeed that Comte himself regarded his plan as an ideal one, to which it was desirable that an approximation should be made, but which he never expected to be fully realised. In criticising it however, little advantage, as it appears to us, can be gained by dwelling only on minor points without endeavouring to convey, in some measure, its aim and spirit. An admirable example of what we consider to be candid and luminous criticism, has been recently furnished by a writer in the Contemporary Review,* who, (in an article entitled 'Aspects of Positivism in relation to Christianity,') has shown a thorough appreciation of the leading ideas and general bearing of Comte's system of religion.

13. It is asserted by the writer in the *National* that Comte was remarkably ignorant 'of Indian worthies and Hindoo institutions.' We are not aware upon what basis this assertion rests, except it be on the fact that Comte has not discussed at length the nature of Hindoo Polytheism. He *has*, in several parts both of the 'Positive Philosophy' and 'Positive Politics,' shown that he was not unacquainted with the Brahminical theocracy, and his appreciation of the caste-system proves, (as we think,) that he must have carefully studied the constitution of society in India as well as in Egypt. Comte had no occasion to enter into any details regarding India,—he had only (1) to indicate summarily the debt owed by Humanity to a race which bequeathed to all future ages the decimal notation in Arithmetic,† and also an Algebra which has afforded to western mathematicians a most powerful instrument of analysis ; and (2) to avail himself in a general way of the lessons which Hindooism offers to the student of Universal History. Comte, although believing that his system might be so modified as to suit the wants of every nation, intended it primarily for what he termed the Western Republic— which consists of the five most advanced and homogeneous nations, namely, France, Italy, Spain, Britain and Germany. The India of the Mahabharata, of the Ramayana, and of Manu's Code, necessarily disappears from Comte's pages with Conservative Polytheism ;—the history of human development is henceforward confined chiefly to the West, and it is there that Comte traces its course from the dawn of Grecian learning through the

---

* See 'Contemporary Review' for July 1868. The article is by the Revd. Brooke F. Westcott.

† See Note A at the end of this Reply.

majestic annals of Rome, the stern discipline of Catholicism and the beautiful conceptions of Chivalry, till it culminates in the science, the industry, and the noble aspirations of Europe in the present century.

It is almost needless to observe that the India of Sanskrit philosophy could only have been introduced by Comte to show the inutility of all metaphysical speculations, a lesson which could be equally well enforced by adducing the unsubstantial theories of German ontologists,

14. "The human mind, by its nature, employs in its progress three methods of philosophising, *the character of which is essentially different.*" It is no valid objection to this proposition, to say that every individual person and nation use the three methods of philosophising. Comte himself has stated the same fact and rests upon it one of the chief arguments in favour of his theory. "The progress of the individual mind," he tells us, "is not only an illustration, but an indirect evidence of that of the general mind. The point of departure of the individual and of the race being the same, the phases of the mind of a man correspond to the epochs of the mind of the race. Now, each of us is aware, if he looks back upon his own history, that he was a theologian in his childhood, a metaphysician in his youth, and a natural philosopher in his manhood." The theological hypothesis is a natural and universal one, it has for long ages been common to the whole human race, and will always remain the starting-point for each individual. History, however, indicates that the advanced races of humanity are gradually losing their primitive beliefs and undergoing an intellectual change, there being observable a constantly growing tendency to push back the supernatural till it becomes a mere abstraction ;—when all that can be predicated of it is, that it is the docile slave of universal Law, thus realising at length the prophetic myth of ancient Greece, that even Zeus himself was bound to obey the decrees of an inexorable Fate. Now each individual in the course of his development must always pass through the same stages that the race itself has passed through ; the rapidity of the advance may be increased, but no essential step can ever be omitted. The development may not be perfect, and the progress in different departments may be effected at different rates, so that the same mind may be, and often is, at the same time,—theological in matters of Faith, metaphysical with reference to social and moral questions, and positive in natural science. The growth of the individual, as, in Comte's opinion, it will hereafter take place, during the completely positive period, is thus characteristically

described:—" In all cases the growth of the individual must, in all essential features, be a reproduction of the growth of the race. You may see, then, that on this point the child must be allowed to obey, unchecked, the general laws that regulate the growth of man's intellect. The first seven years before dentition, he will naturally be fetichist; the next seven till puberty, he will be polytheist. It will be with him as it has been with the race. He will be led by these two philosophical states to begin with developing his powers of observation, then his artistic faculties. As for the questions he may ask his parents, and as for his perceiving that they do not think as he does, there will be no need of any hypocrisy in their answers. This is owing to the relative nature of Positivism. It will be enough, if they openly tell him, that the opinions he has are natural at his age, but that he will come to have others soon, as his parents have done. They may call his attention to the fact that he has already instinctively changed from fetichism to polytheism. He will easily be led to believe that he may change again. And there is no need to hasten the change by artificial means." During the next seven years, while his intellectual powers are being developed by a systematic training, he "will be monotheistic. His monotheism will gradually become simpler and simpler. It will thus be for him, as for the race, a general means of transition to Positivism."

15. We are decidedly of opinion that whatever may have been " the universal tradition regarding the 'golden age' of the world" in times past, that in these later times there has been a very general inclination, quite apart from Comte and his immediate followers, to call in question " the unanimous voice of antiquity attesting the general belief of mankind in a primeval state of light, innocence and truth." But though such scepticism is now general, we believe that no one has done more effectual service than Comte in overthrowing the old doctrine, and in assigning valid arguments for the new one. If we appeal to facts and not to the fictitious dogmas of ancient creeds or the splendid dreams of epic poets, we shall find that the weight of evidence is against the primitive Saturnian reign. All valid evidence, whether à priori or historical, indicates that man commences with a rude kind of theology which has been termed fetichism. "The theological period of humanity" says Comte,[*] "could begin no otherwise than by a complete and usually very durable state of pure fetichism, which allowed free exercise to that tendency

---

[*] "Comte's Positive Philosophy" by Miss Martineau, vol. II, p. 168.

of our nature by which man conceives all external bodies as animated by a life analogous to his own, with differences of mere intensity. This primitive character of human speculation is established by the biological theory of man in the *à priori* way; and in the opposite way, by all the precise information that we can obtain of the earliest social period; and again, the study of individual development confirms the analysis of the collective. Some philosophers set out in the inquiry, as a matter of course, with the supposition that polytheism was the first stage; and some have been so perverse as to place monotheism furthest back, and fetichism as a corruption of polytheism: but such inversions are inconsistent with both the laws and the facts of human history. The real starting point is, in fact, much humbler than is commonly supposed, Man having everywhere begun by being a fetich-worshipper and a cannibal. Instead of indulging our horror and disgust of such a state of things by denying it, we should admit a collective pride in that human progressiveness which has brought us into our present state of comparative exaltation, while a being less nobly endowed than man would have vegetated to this hour in his original wretched condition. Another supposition involves an error less grave, but still requiring notice. Some philosophers suppose a state prior even to fetichism; a state in which the human species was altogether material, and incapable of any speculation whatever;—in that lowest condition in which they now suppose the natives of Tierra del Fuego and some of the Pacific Islanders to be. If this were true, there must have been a time when the intellectual wants did not exist in man; and we must suppose a moment when they began to exist, without any prior manifestation;—a notion which is in direct contradiction to biological principles, which show that the human organism, in all times and places, has manifested the same essential needs, differing only in their degree of development and corresponding mode of satisfaction. This is proof enough of the error of the supposition: and all our observation of the lowest idiotcy and madness, in which man appears to be debased below the higher brutes, assures us that a certain degree of speculative activity exists, which obtains satisfaction in a gross fetichism. On the ground of this hypothesis, it is said that man must have begun like the lower animals. The fact is so,—allowing for superiority of organisation; but perhaps we may find in the defects of the inference a misapprehension of the mental state of the lower animals themselves. Several species of animals afford clear evidence of speculative activity: and those which are endowed with it certainly attain a kind of gross fetichism, as man does,—supposing external bodies, even the most inert, to be animated by passion and will, more or less analogous to the personal impressions of the spectator. The difference in the case is that man has ability to raise himself out of his primitive darkness, and that the brutes have not.* * * It for instance, we exhibit a watch to a child or a savage, on the one hand, and a dog or a monkey on the other, there will be no great difference in their way of regarding the new object, further than their form of expression :—each will suppose it a sort of animal, exercising its own tastes and inclinations ; and in this they will hold a common fetichism,—out of which the one may rise, while the other cannot. * * * It is so difficult for us to conceive of any but a metaphysical theology, that we are apt to fall into perpetual mistakes in contemplating this, its gross origin. Fetichism has been usually confounded with Polytheism, when the latter has been called Idolatry,—a term which applies only to the former. * * * We may recognise some features of that (the fetichistic) state in our own condition of mind when we are betrayed into searching after the mode of production of phenomena, of whose natural laws we are ignorant. We then instinctively conceive of the production of unknown effects according to the passions and affections of the corresponding being regarded as alive ; and this is the philosophical principle of fetichism. A man who smiles at the folly of the savage, in taking the watch for an animal may, if wholly ignorant of watch-making, find himself surprised into a state not so far superior, if any unforeseen and inexplicable effects should arise from some unperceived derangement of the mechanism. But for a widely analogous experience, preparing him for such accidents and their interpretation, he could hardly resist the impression that the changes were tokens of the affections or caprices of an imaginary being."

We hope that the above extract is sufficient to show how far Comte regarded man in his primitive state "as attracted by the idea of universal power over the external world, full of chimerical hopes and exaggerated ideas of his own importance."* In estimating Fetichism he certainly does not treat it as a savage and debasing superstition, but as a phase of belief through which the highest as well as the lowest intellects must pass, and which therefore might manifest itself in the most

---

*This is the language employed by Comte in describing the characteristics of the *theological philosophy.* According to the ancient theology man does not control nature simply by obeying her. Even the Fetichist transfers to the objects of his worship purely human attributes, and thus imposes upon nature his own conditions.

various forms—from the highly poetic fictions of the earliest Aryan races to such gross and realistic conceptions as have been lately disclosed to us so well by Mr. Hunter in his excellent description of the Santhals. "Comte did not" as an eminent English Positivist* has observed, "judge fetichism by the cruelties of African sorcerers, any more than he judged of Catholicism by the cruelties of Spanish inquisitors."

16. The writer in the *National* asserts that although "Astronomy and Natural Science may be said to have passed through a theological stage," yet "the same thing cannot be said of Physics, including Statics and Dynamics ; as Adam Smith remarked, we have never heard of the God of weight, nor have we any more heard of a God of motion." Any difficulty which this remark embodies has been satisfactorily cleared up, to our mind, by Comte himself who argues thus :—"Supreme as the theological philosophy once was, it is certain that such a method of philosophising was resorted to only because no other was possible. Wherever there has been a choice, in regard to any subject whatever, man has always preferred the study of the laws of phenomena to that of their primary causes, though prior training, which there has been no rational education adapted to counteract, has often occasioned lapse into his old illusions. Theological philosophy has, however, never been absolutely universal. That it, the simplest and commonest facts in all classes of phenomena have always been supposed subject to natural laws, and not to the arbitrary will of supernatural agents. Adam Smith made the remark that there never was, in any age or country, a god of weight. In more complex cases, if only the relations of phenomena are seen to be invariable, the most superficial observer recognises the presence of law."† History, it appears to us affords ample evidence that men's physical conceptions were originally theological. "The philosophical speculation of the Greeks," says Mr. Grote,‡ "begins with the theology and cosmology of Homer and Hesiod. The series of divine persons and attributes, and generations, presented by these poets, and especially the Theogony of Hesiod, supplied at one time full satisfaction to the curiosity of the Greeks respecting the past history and present

---

* Dr. J. H. Bridges. See his pamphlet on 'the unity of Comte's life and doctrine,' p. 59.—Fetichism has attained its highest state of development in China. The worship of the followers of Confucius is addressed to Heaven and Earth—the two great Fetiches—and to the Dead. "On the basis of this simple elementary faith" (as Dr. Bridges, in his Essay on *England and China,* well observes) "a rich growth of noble precepts, of glorious memories, of heroic lives, of sacred traditions, was found possible."

† 'Comte's Positive Philosophy' by Miss Martineau. Vol. II. p. 169.

‡ See 'Grote's Plato' Vol. I. p. 2.

agencies of the world around them. * * * * The sentiment of curiosity as it then existed, was only secondary and derivative, arising out of some of the strong primary or personal sentiments—fear or hope, antipathy or sympathy,—impression of present weakness,—unsatisfied appetites and longings—wonder and awe under the presence of the terror-striking phenomena of nature, &c. Under this state of the mind, when problems suggested themselves for solution, the answers afforded by polytheism, gave more satisfaction than could have been afforded by any other hypothesis. Among the indefinite multitude of invisible, impersonal, quasi-human agents, with different attributes and dispositions, some one could be found to account for every perplexing phenomenon. The question asked was not, What are the antecedent conditions and causes of rain, thunder, or earthquakes, but, Who rains and thunders? Who produces earthquakes? The Hesiodic Greek was satisfied when informed that it was Zeus or Poseidon. To be told of physical agencies would have appeared to him not merely unsatisfactory, but absurd, ridiculous, and impious. It was the task of a poet like Hesiod to clothe this general polytheistic sentiment in suitable details; to describe the various gods, goddesses demigods, and other quasi-human agents, with their characteristic attributes, their illustrative adventures, and with sufficient relations of sympathy and subordination among each other, to connect them in men's imaginations as members of the same brotherhood. Okeanus, Gæa, Uranus, Helios, Selenê—Zeus, Poseidon, Hades—Apollo and Artemis, Dionysus and Aphrodite—these and many other divine personal agents, were invoked as the producing and sustaining forces in nature, the past history of which was contained in their filiations or contests."

That physical speculations, when emancipated from purely theological influence, were the chosen arena for à priori notions and metaphysical abstractions, no one who is at all acquainted with the history of human thought would be disposed to deny. Galileo was the first who succeeded in rendering physics definitely positive. "Astronomy," says Comte,* "was a positive science, in its geometrical aspect, from the earliest days of the school of Alexandria; but Physics had no positive character at all till Galileo made his great discoveries on the fall of heavy bodies."

17. The germ of positive Chemistry is found in the doctrine of the four elements which was systematised by Aristotle.† The

---

* 'Comte's Positive Philosophy' by Miss Martineau, Vol. I, p. 215.

† Of course Chemistry must have existed as an art from very early times. The practice of Metallurgy implied a certain amount of Chemical knowledge. The presence, however, of empirical skill in certain arts does not involve more than a very limited amount of positivity in the corresponding sciences.

early Greek schools taught that there was only one elementary substance, but they were not agreed as to their choice of a principle. What notions may have been entertained previously to the rise of the early Greek schools, concerning the composition of terrestrial bodies it may not be easy now to determine, but this much *can* be asserted—that these notions could have been, only in a very limited sense, *scientific*. Alchemy is the form under which Chemistry was developed during the middle ages, and in its peculiar doctrines may be traced the influence of theological as well as metaphysical modes of thought. "Like all other kinds of mysticism," says Dr. Whewell,* "alchemy seems to have grown out of the notions of moral, personal, and mythological qualities, which men associated with terms, of which the primary application was to physical properties."

It must not be imagined, as the writer in the *National* seems to imply, that a department of human thought becomes positive immediately after a germ of science has sprung up within it. The three modes of conception indicated by Comte generally co-exist, so that it will in most cases be found that a particular subject is not wholly in any one stage, but merely that the *prevailing* tenour of its speculations is either theological, or metaphysical, or positive. In assigning, therefore, the category to which a subject at any one time ought to belong, it is only with its *most marked characteristics* that we are concerned, and these are determined partly by the general state of development of the human mind, and partly by the nature of the subject itself—those subjects which are least complex arriving at positivity most speedily. Where the *general* tone of thought is theological or metaphysical, old modes of belief will continue to linger even after a department has been rendered thoroughly positive.

18. The writer in the *National*, following in the footsteps of Mr. Mill, has endeavoured to throw ridicule upon Comte's positive idealisation. As Dr. Bridges, in his pamphlet on 'the Unity of Comte's Life and Doctrine,' has offered a most satisfactory and forcible answer to Mr. Mill's strictures, we shall here simply reproduce his language:—"That aspect of Positivism which he (Comte) thought assimilable to Fetichism was the tendency, developed exceptionally in Chinese civilisation, and visible in the primitive history of other nations, to endow the visible world with human emotions and sympathies. That ardent love of nature so distinctive of modern feeling, that yearning to endow the earth, sea, and sky with passions corresponding to our own, which penetrates the painting of Turner, and the poetry of Shelley,

* 'History of the Inductive Sciences,' Vol. I, p. 303.

is something which, amidst the prosaic perplexities and artificial dulness of modern life, reunites us with the early memories of childhood, rekindles the ancient vigour, and renovates the long-lost freshness of primeval centuries. What Wordsworth expressed in his Ode on Immortality, or Shelley in the Earth-hymn of his " Prometheus Unbound," Comte has expressed, in his own way, in the *Synthèse Subjective*. * * * The utility of adorning science, its accuracy being sternly defended, with a fringe of beautiful imaginations, and so preserving the artistic habit of mind unimpaired amidst the dangers inseparable from analytic thought, is a large question, which need not be discussed here."

19. Comte's views on Optics.—It is well known that Comte rejected the undulatory theory of Light. According to the writer in the *National*, if this theory be not adopted, there can be no positive science of Optics, in as much as the *facts* cannot be expressed or conceived without it. Comte appears to have been of a different opinion,* though his views may not be worth much in the estimation of one who endorses Dr. Whewell's assertions that Comte was " ignorant of modern optics", and that " the language in which he speaks of all modern sciences, except astronomy, is that of a shallow pretender, using general phrases in the attempt to make his expressions seem to be knowledge." It is much to be regretted that a man of Dr. Whewell's magnificent attainments should have spoken in such terms of one who is allowed, even by the generality of his adversaries, to rank among the profoundest thinkers of either ancient or modern times. If Comte was such a charlatan as Dr. Whewell makes him out to be, it is strange that his doctrines should have been thought worthy of notice at all in a treatise which claims the merit of unfolding *the* philosophy of the inductive sciences.

Comte did not, however, reject the undulatory hypothesis without assigning very good reasons for the course he adopted. Starting from the fundamental principle that science deals only with the laws of phenomena, he was led to construct certain canons for the formation of valid *hypotheses*. " There are only two general methods" he tells us,† " by which we can get at the law of any phenomenon,—the immediate analysis of the course of the phenomenon, or its relation to some more extended law

---

* He says, " the history of Optics, regarded as a whole, seems to show that these hypotheses have not sensibly aided the progress of the theory of light, since all our important acquisitions have been entirely independent of them."—Positive Philosophy, Vol. I, p. 267.

† 'Positive Philosophy' by Miss. Martineau. Vol. I. p. 224.

already established; in other words, by induction or deduction. Neither of these methods would help us, even in regard to the simplest phenomena, if we did not begin by anticipating the results, by making a provisional supposition, altogether conjectural in the first instance, with regard to some of the very notions which are the object of the inquiry. Hence the necessary introduction of hypotheses into natural philosophy. The method of approximation employed by geometers first suggested the idea; and without it all discovery of natural laws would be impossible in cases of any degree of complexity; and in all, very slow. But the employment of this instrument must always be subjected to one condition, the neglect of which would impede the development of real knowledge. This condition is to imagine such hypotheses only as admit, by their nature, of a positive and inevitable verification at some future time, the precision of this verification being proportioned to what we can learn of the corresponding phenomena. In other words, philosophical hypotheses must always have the character of simple anticipations of what we might know at once, by experiment and reasoning, if the circumstances of the problem had been more favourable than they are."

Having thus indicated the nature of legitimate hypotheses, he proceeds to observe:—"The hypotheses employed by physical inquirers in our day are of two classes: the first, a very small class, relate simply to the laws of phenomena: the other, and larger class, aim at determining the general agents to which different kinds of natural effects may be referred. Now, according to the rule just laid down, the first kind alone are admissible: the second have an unscientific character, are chimerical, and can do nothing but hinder the progress of science."

Among hypotheses belonging to the second class, Comte places both the emission and undulatory theories of light. Alluding to the two schools which have adopted these respective doctrines, he remarks:—"Each has exposed the untenableness of the doctrines held by the other; and each explorer has confined himself to the evidence which favoured his own conception. Euler brought fatal objections against the doctrine of emission; yet, at the present day, our instructors conceal the fact that the advocates of the emission doctrine have offered equally fatal objections to that of undulation. * * * The case is made clearer by the fact that there are phenomena which the two theories will suit equally well. If the laws of reflection and refraction issue with equal ease from the hypotheses of emission and undulation, it is pretty clear that our business is with the laws, and not with the hypotheses."

Mr. Mill, whom the writer in the *National* appears inclined to regard as an authority, has accepted Comte's canons of hypothesis in their integrity, and has sustained them, in his own clear way, with a wealth of argument and illustration. Speaking of the supposed luminiferous ether, he observes*, " It can never be brought to the test of observation, because the ether is supposed wanting in all the properties by means of which our senses take cognisance of external phenomena. It can neither be seen, heard, smelt, tasted, nor touched. The possibility of deducing from its supposed laws a considerable number of the phenomena of light, is the sole evidence of its existence that we have ever to hope for; and this evidence cannot be of the smallest value, because we cannot have, in the case of such an hypothesis, the assurance that if the hypothesis be false, it must lead to results at variance with the true facts." Such is the estimate of Comte's views on this subject, as given by one who, we believe, has not yet been branded as a shallow pretender, and as ignorant of almost every science; by one who, in India if not elsewhere, is regarded as the keenest of thinkers, the foremost of philanthropists:—and hence we trust that his approval may redeem Comte, in the estimation of our Indian readers, from the flippant accusations indulged in by the distinguished metaphysical historian of the inductive sciences.

It is hardly necessary to notice the statement that Comte excluded " all *scientific* theories from positive science," as it will be evident from what has been said above, that he gave a wide latitude in the construction of hypotheses, that he considered a legitimate hypothesis *essential* for the collection and arrangement of facts in order that they might lead to definite results, and that he accordingly welcomed with enthusiasm any theory which was really *scientific*.

20. Comte's views on Geology.—Even allowing that Geology is a science of equal definiteness with Mineralogy or Botany, it must nevertheless have been excluded from Comte's classification which has reference only to those sciences which deal with the fundamental and elementary laws of phenomena. The division of sciences into *abstract* and *concrete* is one of Comte's most luminous conceptions, and he shows clearly enough that, in organising a Philosophy or general doctrine, he has only to deal with the former class. The distinction is thus clearly pointed out, at the commencement of the ' Positive Philosophy' :—" One more preliminary remark occurs, before we finish the prescription

---

* Mill's Logic Vol. II. p. 22, second edition.

of our limits,—the ascertainment of our field of inquiry. We must distinguish between the two classes of natural science; the abstract or general, which have for their object the discovery of the laws which regulate phenomena in all conceivable cases: and the concrete, particular, or descriptive, which are sometimes called natural sciences in a restricted sense, whose function it is to apply these laws to the actual history of existing beings. The first are fundamental; and our business is with them alone, as the second are derived, and however important, not rising into the rank of our subjects of contemplation. We shall treat of physiology, but not of botany and zoology, which are derived from it. We shall treat of chemistry, but not of mineralogy, which is secondary to it."

But as regards Geology, it is perfectly true that Comte did not consider the heterogeneous mass of materials included under that name as entitled to form a distinct concrete science. Not only is Geology mixed up with crude hypotheses which, as the Rev. Mr. Baden Powell observes,* "might not unnaturally have influenced him (Comte) in entertaining a prejudice against it," but it is also, as the same writer has justly hinted, wanting in that "perfect definiteness of the conceptions involved" which would entitle it to rank with such subjects as Mineralogy, Botany, or Zoology. Even a cursory examination of any of the ordinary treatises on Geology will be sufficient to show that the researches entered into are of the most indefinite character, and that so far from constituting any one science they range over a number of distinct departments and are bound together by no common tie. So vague is the term that a work on Geology might, without doing violence to established usage, be made to include almost the whole cycle of speculation—from geometry up to the primeval history of man himself.

21. The writer in the *National* quotes a sentence of Mr. Mill's regarding Comte's sociology, to the following effect :—" He (Comte) has done nothing in sociology which does not require to be done over again and better." This is given, as we have stated it, without any qualification, so that the reader would probably conclude that Mr. Mill considers Comte's sociological investigations as of very little worth. We have not Mr. Mill's two essays (first published in the *Westminster Review*,) now at hand, but if our memory does not betray us the sentence above

---

* See 'Powell's Unity of Worlds,' pp. 55, 548.—To the orthodox Geologist we recommend the perusal of Mr. Herbert Spencer's Essay on 'Illogical Geology.'

quoted has reference more especially to that portion of the subject which Comte termed *statical* sociology.* Mr. Mill may not perhaps agree with all the conclusions at which Comte has arrived with reference to history or dynamical sociology, yet it is certain that in his 'System of Logic' he has highly eulogised Comte's method and the scientific character of his conclusions. He says, " M. Comte alone, among the new historical school, has seen the necessity of connecting all our generalisations from history with the laws of human nature ; and he alone, therefore, has arrived at any results truly scientific." Again, "his (Comte's) works are hitherto the only known example of the study of social phenomena on the true principles of the Historical Method. Of that method I do not hesitate to pronounce them a model." Speaking of the 'law of the three stages,' Mr. Mill remarks :— "This generalisation appears to me to have that high degree of scientific evidence, which is derived from the concurrence of the indications of history with the probabilities derived from the constitution of the human mind. Nor could it be easily con- ceived, from the mere enunciation of such a proposition, what a flood of light it lets in upon the whole course of history ; when its consequences are traced by connecting it with each of the three states of human intellect which it distinguishes, and with each successive modification of those three states, the corre- lative condition of all other social phenomena."

22. According to the writer in the *National* " Comte says that not only do all the sciences, properly so called, pass through three successive stages, but he affirms the same of each of our leading conceptions." It appears to us that this language indicates a misapprehension as to what Comte really meant by our *leading conceptions*. The law of the three stages, says Comte, " consists in this, that each of our principal conceptions, each branch of know- ledge passes successivly through three different theoretical states —the theological or fictitious state, the metaphysical or abstract state, and the scientific or positive state." Now here as elsewhere he employs *principal conceptions* as synonomous with *sciences*. His encyclopædic scale of sciences was also termed by him the Theoretical Hierarchy of human conceptions—these fundamental conceptions including (1) Number, Extension, and Motion, (2) Matter—in its Astromical, Physical, and Chemical aspects,—(3) Life, (4) and lastly Man—in his Social and Moral relations. As however all our other theoretical conceptions depend upon these primary ones, it would be quite right to assert, without any

limitation, that *every* theoretical conception is subject to Comte's great law of mental development.

Comte, it may be here observed, is of opinion that all knowledge which is calculated to have a really beneficial effect upon practice, may and eventually will be rendered completely positive. Hence if there is, as the writer in the *National* maintains, any knowledge which " must for ever remain in that vague and indistinct state in which all scientific knowledge originally was," Positivism would discourage its reception as tending to lead us astray, and to withdraw the mind from inquiries which experience has shown to be both intelligible and remunerative.

23. That there are phenomena of mind which must be observed and co-ordinated, Comte himself readily admitted, but he did not allow that *internal consciousness* could be relied upon as a trustworthy guide in our investigations. Enough has been said on this subject in a pamphlet lately published by us on ' Comte and the Metaphysicians,' to which we must refer our readers for arguments against the employment of self-consciousness as an instrument of psychological investigation.

24. Logic is regarded by Comte not as a special science, but rather as that without which science of any kind would be impossible—namely, a vehicle for the discovery of truth. The Logic of a Science is the apparatus of mental artifices adapted for investigating the subject matter to which the science refers. Hence Logic has several organa, or to use a familiar metaphor, it is like a knife with many blades, each one adapted for cutting a different material. In Mathematics logic is purely *deductive* : that is, deduction is the instrument with which the mind works in the co-ordination of Mathematical truth. In Astronomy the Logic of *observation* comes into play, in Terrestrial Physics we employ chiefly the Logic of *experiment.* Biology developes the Logic of *Comparison.* In establishing Sociology, Logic requires an additional instrument, namely *Historical Filiation.* Thus then the Positive Method is fully constituted, and hence it appears that to understand Logic in its integrity, the student must be conversant with the distinctive processes of all the fundamental sciences. " To learn reasoning," says Comte, " the only way is to reason with certainty and precision on clear and definite matter. Many who are quite aware that to learn an art, you must practise that art, still listen to the sophists who teach them to reason, or even to speak, by reasoning on reasoning, or by speaking about speech. * * * Each essential branch of the Positive Method must always be studied in the particular department of science which gave occasion to its introduction."

25.   Comte does not exclude Ethics from the series of Positive Sciences.   A glance at the Encyclopedic Scale, published in the Positivist Catechism, will show that Morals is included as a branch of Sociology.   "At the highest point of the encyclopedic scale," says Comte, "I place *Moral Science,* or the science of the individual man.   * * * As a fact, morals, the most useful of all the sciences, is also the most complete, or rather it is the only one which is complete, since its phenomena subjectively embrace all the others, though, by that very fact, they are objectively subordinate to these others.   The fundamental principle of the scientific hierarchy gives a direct predominance to the moral point of view as the most complicated and special."

It is true that in the 'Positive Philosophy' morals is not noticed as a distinct science.   But it is easy to explain the omission. The object of the Positive Philosophy was to discover the laws of our *intellectual* and *active* development.   In such an investigation it was not necessary to discuss man's moral nature (otherwise than incidentally,) because, although feeling is superior to both intellect and action in dignity, yet it is subordinate to them in respect of its growth.   According to Comte's cerebral theory,* "the affective region of the brain has no direct communication with the external world.   The latter influences the former through the intervention of the intellectual and active organs. Thus the mutual influence of families and generations cannot directly modify our inclinations : it can only affect them by the changes which it works in our thoughts and actions.   If our intellectual and practical condition were to remain unchanged, no alteration could take place in our moral state.   * * * Reciprocally, our inclinations only affect our social evolution by modifying our opinions and our conduct.   The whole normal advance of humanity, therefore, bears directly only upon our intellect and activity".

26.   The writer in the *National* asserts that Comte virtually excluded from the series of positive sciences not only Logic and Ethics but also Ideology and Æsthetics.   As we are ignorant of the exact nature of Ideology† we cannot decide whether it is virtually included in Comte's classification or not; but we are confident that, although Æsthetics will not be found in the 'Hierarchy of Human Conceptions', Positivism has made ample

---

* 'Politique Positive,' vol. III p. 11.

† If 'Ideology' is but another name for 'Mental Science,' then Comte has (in our opinion) made ample provision for it.   Biology and Morals are both concerned with investigations regarding the mind of man ; History also discloses certain great intellectual laws.

provision for the æsthetical side of human nature. In his 'General View of Positivism' Comte writes thus :*—"In the normal state of our nature it (Reason) has also another function ; that of regulating and stimulating Imagination, without yielding passive obedience to it. The æsthetic faculties are far too important to be disregarded in the normal state of Humanity; therefore they must not be omitted from the system which aims to introduce that state. There is a strong but groundless prejudice that in this respect at least Positivism will be found wanting. Yet it furnishes the only true foundation of modern Art, which, since the Middle Ages, has been cultivated without fixed principles or lofty purpose."

27. Whether or not Positivism is, as the writer in the *National* asserts, a mutilated form of 'Kant's Critical Philosophy,' is a matter which we must leave our readers to decide for themselves. Our knowledge of Kant's writings is not sufficiently extensive to justify us in instituting a comparison between the *critical* and the *positive* philosophies. Comte, however, has freely acknowledged the debt which he owes to the great German ; though not to the extent which would induce us to conclude that Positivism was merely such a crude plagiarism as the writer in the *National* would lead his readers to suppose. "Sprung" says Comte, "from this great stock (the school of Diderot and Hume) historically, I have never scrupled to connect with it whatever of real eminence our latest adversaries have produced, whether of the theological or metaphysical school. Hume is my principal precursor in philosophy, but with Hume I connect Kant as an accessory. Kant's fundamental conception was never really systematised and developed but by Positivism." The fundamental conception here alluded to is 'the distinction between objective and subjective reality.' Positivism, according to Comte, gives the conception its full value by connecting it with the general biological law— that every organism is in a constant dependence on the sum of external influences.

28. Many of the points raised in the fifth article of the *National* have already been discussed in the pamphlet† to which we have before alluded, and to it we must refer those of our readers who are curious upon such matters.

The writer in the *National* informs us, towards the close of his remarks, that we may legitimately pass from phenomena which

---

* Translated by Dr. Bridges, see p. 291.
† 'Comte and the Metaphysicians' by a Positivist.

are effects to antecedent phenomena which have a *potency** to produce these effects, and thence to marks of design, intelligence and goodness, and finally from such marks to an intelligent, wise, and good Creator : but he will not allow us " to reverse the process and from our belief in a Creator to reason downwards with a view of discovering the character of the phenomena." No reasons are assigned for this arbitrary veto, and if none *can* be assigned we must persist in our belief that the interdiction of the second method is a sign of the untrustworthiness of the first. If we really knew the Deity, not metaphysically, but as revelation unfolds him to our view, then surely we might reason from the author to the nature of the work, as well as from the work to the nature of its author. If Theology be trustworthy, Metaphysics must be needless ; if Metaphysics can unfold the veil, Theology is superseded.

29. Dr. Whewell (says the writer in the *National*) asks, " Are all chemical compounds binary ? M. Comte thinks they are : a metaphysical doctrine surely for he gives no physical reason for it." As we do not pretend to be an authority on chemical science, we shall simply state Comte's reason in his own language, without adding any criticism of our own :—" The sum of what has been said on this important subject of chemical dualism is this :—the real mode of agglomeration of elementary particles is, and ever must be, unknown to us, and therefore no proper object of our study—our positive researches being thus circumscribed, we may rationally conceive of the *immediate* composition of any substance as binary ; but so as to represent all the phenomena that chemistry can offer to us, in any future state of perfection. Thus, I do not propose universal dualism as a law of nature ; for this we could never establish : but I do declare it to be a fundamental artifice of true chemical philosophy, destined to simplify our elementary conceptions, by using our optional intellectual liberty in accordance with the true end and aim of positive chemistry." Thus it will be seen that Comte did not introduce *chemical dualism* as a metaphysical idea, but merely as a convenient and legitimate hypothesis.

30. " What conception" asks the writer in the *National* " can we have of Statics or Dynamics without an idea of force ?—but force is a metaphysical idea not within the province of Positive Science, if metaphysics be excluded." Now in reply to this we have no hesitation in saying that the idea of force,

---

* May we ask if *potency* belongs to the consequent as well as the antecedent? The question is not an unimportant one.

as a metaphysical conception, is in no way necessary to the truths of Statics and Dynamics. In these sciences *force* is merely used as an abbreviated expression for 'motion, change of motion, or tendency to motion.' Of force as a separate entity, or as an *ultimate* cause of motion, we know nothing ; as the subject of science it can only be known by the phenomena which it produces. In Dynamics where force is measured directly by the motion produced, the artificial nature of the conception is so apparent that it is the fashion now-a-days to preface treatises on Dynamics with what is termed Kinematics, or the science of pure motion, in which the problems of Dynamics are worked out without introducing the idea of force at all.*

Force and other such like terms when employed simply as bonds to connect external facts, are in no proper sense metaphysical. They are subjective, it may be, but they rest upon a sufficient objective basis to warrant their admission within the domain of positive science.†

31. In concluding these remarks, we would observe that although the writer in the *National* has insisted strongly on the validity of metaphysical speculations, he has not told his readers to which of the many metaphysical schools he himself belongs. He has mentioned with a certain amount of approbation Leibnitz, Descartes, Bacon, Locke, Berkeley, Kant, Whewell, and Mill, but he has not indicated to which of these philosophers we are to look for a consistent and reliable system which may serve us as a constant guide amidst the conflicts of opinion by which we are now surrounded. To those who read these pages we can recommend Positivism, with all confidence, both from a *speculative* and *practical* point of view, and we trust that all such will not rest content with any partial notices, either favorable or hostile, but will have recourse, if possible, to the fountain-head, so as to judge for themselves the validity of the claim which Comte has put forth, to found a doctrine which should inaugurate a new era in the history of man—a bold claim it is true, but one which, owing to the reputation of its author, deserves a careful and dispassionate consideration.

---

* We have no idea of Force *per se :* Force is known only by certain effects produced. In Mechanics, *motion* is the effect considered, and Force is defined as 'Whatever produces or tends to produce change in a body's state of rest or motion. Hence, from a *mechanical point of view*, Pressure, Gravity, Friction, Electricity Magnetism, &c., may all be regarded as identical.

† See Note C at the end of this Reply.

Note A.

Max Müller thus extols the service which the Hindoos have rendered to science by their admirable arithmetical notation :—"It would be highly important to find out at what time the nought occurs for the first time in Indian inscriptions. That inscription would deserve to be preserved among the most valuable monuments of antiquity, for from it would date in reality the beginning of true mathematical science, impossible without the nought—nay, the beginning of all the exact sciences to which we owe the discoveries of telescopes, steam-engines, and electric-telegraphs." Although this is certainly not the language of a mathematician, yet it manifests a thoroughly just appreciation of the share which the Hindoos have had in contributing to man's intellectual progress. To many the terms employed may appear exaggerated, but it must be remembered that long familiarity with the gifts of past ages has rendered it very difficult for us to appreciate rightly the efforts made by the early pioneers of human thought.

Note B.

We have since procured a copy of Mr. Mill's articles on 'Auguste Comte and Positivism'; and, on referring to the passage alluded to by the writer in the *National*, we find that our interpretation is not altogether correct. As Mr. Mill's censure, however, is accompanied by an important qualification, it may be as well to give the passage in full. "Meanwhile" says Mr. Mill "the reader will gather, from what has been said, that M. Comte has not, in our opinion, created Sociology. Except his analysis of history, to which there is much to be added, but which we do not think likely to be ever, in its general features, superseded, he has done nothing in Sociology which does not require to be done over again, and better. Nevertheless he has greatly advanced the study. Besides the great stores of thought, of various and often of eminent merit, with which he has enriched the subject, his conception of its method is so much truer and more profound than that of any one who preceded him, as to constitute an era in its cultivation."

How Mr. Mill manages to reconcile a belief in the eminent merit of Comte's historical analysis, with a belief in the utter worthlessness of the Positive Sociology it is not for us to determine. Comte, as we think, has done a signal service to mankind by simply hazarding a solution of the most important social and moral questions. While his followers regard the work of their master as to a great extent definitive, his impartial adversaries might at least award him praise for having attempted such a task at all—remembering that in every department of human thought successful results can only be obtained after many trials and repeated failures. Mr. Mill, it appears to us, has not sufficiently recognised Comte's claims to our gratitude even if the experience of after ages should prove his system to be only a splendid Utopia.

Note C.

The writer in the *National*, while dilating upon the services which certain metaphysical philosophers have rendered to the cause of science, observes that "it is the Metaphysical Logic discarded by Comte that enables *him* to discover the *illogical* character of the Differential Calculus." This statement can involve no charge against Comte unless the writer means to assert that the intellectual processes with which Logic deals are purely metaphysical.

It appears, from recent controversies, that a certain class of critics insist upon characterising the mental element of our knowledge as *metaphysical*. To such critics we can only say that they employ the term *metaphysical* in a sense very different from that which Comte attached to it. With Comte a conception was metaphysical when it claimed to be *purely* subjective, resting upon no concrete basis and therefore incapable of verification.

As regards the Scholastic Logic, we readily allow that Comte had no very high opinion of the benefits that can *now* result from a study of that so-called science. Such a study may be useful historically, but it is almost worthless for teaching men how to reason. With Comte, Logic is more of an art than a science; and as an art can only be learnt by practice, so Logic can only be learnt by reasoning upon some well-defined and appropriate matter. Hence in order to appreciate the deductive Logic thoroughly, Mathematics—the essentially deductive science—must be mastered.

So far as the Scholastic Logic merely analyses the mental processes employed in reasoning, it is explicit and intelligible enough, though, as we think, not very profitable. It is only when Logic attempts to investigate mind as an entity or essence, that it can be regarded as strictly metaphysical, and when so employed we are confident that it can lead to no solid results :—that it could ever enable any one to detect a theoretical flaw in a mathematical method of proof is what even the most strenuous opponents of Positivism, we imagine, would be hardly prepared to maintain.

This is not the place to enter into the technicalities of mathematics, but it is well-known to all who have studied the Differential Calculus how desirable it is that the fundamental artifice upon which that science depends should be placed upon a satisfactory logical basis. Three distinct methods have been employed for solving that particular class of problems with which the Differential Calculus deals. These are (1) the *infinitesimal* method, (2) the method of *limits*, and (3) the method of *derived functions*. Comte regards the *first* of these methods as illogical, but distinct and precise : the *second* as logical, but comparatively weak in resources and embarrassing in operation ; the *third* as the most philosophical of the three, combining perfect unity of analysis with a purely abstract character in the fundamental ideas involved.

www.ingramcontent.com/pod-product-compliance
Lightning Source LLC
Chambersburg PA
CBHW081303040426
42452CB00014B/2636